# EMMANUEL JOSEPH

# Security Economics

*Copyright © 2023 by Emmanuel Joseph*

*All rights reserved. No part of this publication may be reproduced, stored or transmitted in any form or by any means, electronic, mechanical, photocopying, recording, scanning, or otherwise without written permission from the publisher. It is illegal to copy this book, post it to a website, or distribute it by any other means without permission.*

*First edition*

*This book was professionally typeset on Reedsy. Find out more at reedsy.com*

# Contents

| | | |
|---|---|---|
| 1 | Introduction to Security Economics | 1 |
| 2 | The Economics of Threats and Vulnerabilities | 5 |
| 3 | Cost-Benefit Analysis in Security | 9 |
| 4 | Risk Management and Insurance | 13 |
| 5 | Investment Strategies for Security | 16 |
| 6 | Regulation and Compliance | 20 |
| 7 | Security in Supply Chains | 24 |
| 8 | Human Factors in Security Economics | 28 |
| 9 | Security in the Internet of Things (IoT) | 32 |
| 10 | Economic Impacts of Security Breaches | 36 |
| 11 | Emerging Trends in Security Economics | 41 |
| 12 | Strategic Decision-Making in Security Economics | 45 |

# 1

# Introduction to Security Economics

Security Economics is a multidisciplinary field that blends the principles of economics with the complex and ever-evolving world of security. This chapter serves as a foundational exploration into the concepts, significance, and key elements of security economics.

1.1 Defining Security Economics

Security economics is the systematic study of how individuals, organizations, and societies make decisions about allocating resources to protect against risks, threats, and vulnerabilities. It applies economic principles, such as cost-benefit analysis and risk management, to the realm of security. In essence, it seeks to answer critical questions, including:

- How much should be invested in security measures?
    - What is the economic impact of security breaches?
    - How can limited resources be optimally allocated for security?

1.2 Importance of Security Economics

Understanding security economics is essential in today's interconnected and digital world. Security incidents, whether in the form of cyberattacks, physical breaches, or supply chain disruptions, can have far-reaching economic consequences. Consider these key reasons for the importance of security economics:

### 1.2.1 Risk Management

Security economics provides a structured framework for assessing, mitigating, and managing risks. By quantifying potential losses and evaluating the cost-effectiveness of security measures, organizations can make informed decisions about how to protect their assets.

### 1.2.2 Resource Allocation

Resources for security are finite, and allocating them efficiently is paramount. Security economics helps organizations strike a balance between investing in security and achieving other business objectives. It guides decision-makers in prioritizing security investments based on their economic impact.

### 1.2.3 Regulatory Compliance

Many industries are subject to government regulations related to security and privacy. Compliance with these regulations often involves significant costs. Security economics assists organizations in assessing the economic implications of compliance and determining the most cost-effective ways to meet regulatory requirements.

### 1.2.4 Technological Advancements

As technology evolves, so do security threats and vulnerabilities. Security economics helps organizations adapt to new challenges by evaluating the economics of emerging security technologies and strategies.

## 1.3 Overview of Key Concepts

# INTRODUCTION TO SECURITY ECONOMICS

Before delving deeper into security economics, it's crucial to grasp several foundational concepts:

### 1.3.1 Cost-Benefit Analysis (CBA)

Cost-benefit analysis is a fundamental tool in security economics. It involves comparing the costs of implementing security measures to the expected benefits, which may include risk reduction, potential savings from preventing incidents, and enhanced reputation. CBA helps organizations make rational decisions about security investments.

### 1.3.2 Risk Assessment

Risk assessment is the process of identifying, evaluating, and prioritizing security risks. Security economics employs risk assessment to quantify the likelihood and potential impact of various threats, enabling organizations to allocate resources effectively.

### 1.3.3 Security Investment Strategies

Organizations must determine how much to invest in security. Security economics explores various investment strategies, such as proactive vs. reactive security measures, and examines the trade-offs between security costs and benefits.

### 1.3.4 Human Factors

Human behavior plays a crucial role in security. Understanding the economic aspects of human factors, such as employee training, awareness programs, and the costs associated with insider threats, is essential in security economics.

### 1.3.5 Emerging Trends

Security economics is not static. It evolves alongside technological advancements, regulatory changes, and shifting threat landscapes. This chapter provides an introduction to the dynamic nature of security economics and foreshadows the exploration of future trends in subsequent chapters.

In summary, security economics is an interdisciplinary field that combines economic principles with security challenges. It addresses the critical need for efficient resource allocation, risk management, and decision-making in an increasingly complex security landscape. This introductory chapter sets the stage for a comprehensive exploration of security economics in the chapters to follow.

# 2

# The Economics of Threats and Vulnerabilities

In this chapter, we dive deeper into the core concepts of security economics by focusing on the economic aspects of threats and vulnerabilities. Understanding the economics behind threats and vulnerabilities is essential for making informed decisions about security investments, risk management, and resource allocation.

2.1 Understanding Cyber Threats

2.1.1 Threat Landscape Analysis

The first section of this chapter delves into the diverse and ever-evolving landscape of cyber threats. It explores various types of threats, from malware and phishing attacks to advanced persistent threats (APTs). Understanding the economic motivations behind these threats is crucial, as threat actors often seek financial gain, political objectives, or other incentives.

2.1.2 Threat Actors and Economics

This subsection explores the motivations and economic incentives of threat actors, including cybercriminals, hacktivists, and state-sponsored entities. Examining the economics of threat actors helps us comprehend their decision-making processes and adapt security strategies accordingly.

### 2.1.3 Economic Impact of Cyber Threats

Quantifying the economic impact of cyber threats is challenging but essential. This section explores methodologies for estimating the costs associated with data breaches, system downtime, reputational damage, and other consequences of security incidents.

## 2.2 Assessing Vulnerabilities

### 2.2.1 Vulnerability Analysis

Vulnerabilities are weaknesses in systems or processes that can be exploited by threats. This section delves into vulnerability assessment methods, highlighting the economic importance of identifying and addressing vulnerabilities proactively.

### 2.2.2 Vulnerability Exploitation Economics

Understanding how threat actors exploit vulnerabilities for economic gain is essential for prioritizing security measures. This part of the chapter explores the economics of vulnerability exploitation, including the costs and benefits for attackers.

### 2.2.3 Risk Exposure and Vulnerability Management

Organizations face risks associated with vulnerabilities. This section introduces the concept of risk exposure and explains how organizations can use economic models to manage vulnerabilities cost-effectively.

## 2.3 Economic Impacts of Security Breaches

### 2.3.1 Direct Costs of Security Breaches

Security breaches come with tangible costs, such as incident response, data recovery, and legal expenses. This section explores these direct costs and how organizations can estimate them.

### 2.3.2 Indirect Costs and Reputational Damage

Beyond direct costs, security breaches can lead to indirect costs, including loss of customer trust and damaged reputation. Analyzing the economic impact of these intangible factors is crucial for understanding the full scope of security incidents.

### 2.3.3 Long-Term Consequences

Security breaches often have long-term economic consequences, such as increased insurance premiums and the need for ongoing security enhancements. This section examines the long-term financial implications of security incidents.

## 2.4 Case Studies and Examples

Throughout the chapter, real-world case studies and examples illustrate the economic principles discussed. These cases showcase how organizations have grappled with threats, vulnerabilities, and security breaches from an economic perspective.

## 2.5 Conclusion

Chapter 2 concludes by emphasizing the importance of understanding the economics of threats and vulnerabilities in the context of security. It highlights the role of this knowledge in informed decision-making, risk management, and resource allocation. The chapter also sets the stage for subsequent chapters, which will explore cost-benefit analysis, risk management strategies, and the economic aspects of security regulation and compliance.

# 3

# Cost-Benefit Analysis in Security

Cost-benefit analysis (CBA) is a fundamental tool in security economics that allows organizations to evaluate security investments by comparing the costs of implementing security measures to the expected benefits. In this chapter, we explore how CBA is applied in the context of security and its role in informed decision-making.

3.1 Introduction to Cost-Benefit Analysis

3.1.1 What is Cost-Benefit Analysis?

This section provides a concise definition of CBA and its origins in economics. It outlines the basic principles of CBA, which involve comparing the total costs of an action or project to the total benefits it generates.

3.1.2 The Role of CBA in Security

Here, we establish the significance of CBA in security. CBA helps organizations make rational and data-driven decisions about security investments, allowing them to allocate resources effectively and maximize their security posture.

## 3.2 Conducting Cost-Benefit Analysis in Security

### 3.2.1 Identifying Costs

This subsection explains how to identify and categorize costs associated with security measures. It includes direct costs like purchasing security software and indirect costs like employee training and the opportunity cost of resources spent on security.

### 3.2.2 Estimating Benefits

Estimating the benefits of security measures can be complex. This section explores various aspects of benefits, including risk reduction, potential savings from preventing security incidents, and intangible benefits like enhanced reputation and customer trust.

### 3.2.3 Quantifying Risk Reduction

Quantifying risk reduction is a crucial part of CBA in security. Techniques such as risk assessment models and probabilistic analysis are discussed, along with their application in estimating the economic value of risk mitigation.

## 3.3 Practical Applications of CBA in Security

### 3.3.1 Prioritizing Security Investments

One of the primary applications of CBA in security is prioritizing investments. This section explains how organizations can use CBA to compare the economic value of different security measures and allocate resources to the most cost-effective options.

### 3.3.2 Cost-Effective Security Strategies

Organizations often face budget constraints. CBA helps them determine the most cost-effective security strategies that provide the best return on investment (ROI) in terms of risk reduction and other benefits.

### 3.3.3 Case Studies and Examples

Throughout this chapter, we present real-world case studies and examples that illustrate how CBA has been applied successfully in various security scenarios. These cases provide insights into the practical challenges and benefits of using CBA for security decision-making.

## 3.4 Challenges and Limitations of CBA in Security

### 3.4.1 Uncertainty and Assumptions

CBA in security is not without its challenges. This section discusses the uncertainty and assumptions involved in estimating costs and benefits, highlighting the importance of sensitivity analysis.

### 3.4.2 Intangible Benefits and Externalities

Not all benefits of security measures are easily quantifiable. Intangible benefits and externalities, such as improved brand image and reduced societal security risks, can be challenging to measure but should be considered in CBA.

### 3.4.3 Ethical and Moral Considerations

Security decisions can have ethical and moral implications, and CBA may not capture all these factors. Organizations must consider ethical considerations when conducting CBA for security.

## 3.5 Conclusion

Chapter 3 concludes by underscoring the importance of cost-benefit analysis in security economics. It highlights how CBA empowers organizations to make informed decisions about security investments, manage risks effectively, and optimize resource allocation. As we progress through the book, subsequent chapters will explore other key aspects of security economics, including risk management, security regulation and compliance, and emerging trends in the field.

# 4

# Risk Management and Insurance

In the realm of security economics, managing risks and considering insurance strategies is paramount. This chapter delves into the intricacies of risk assessment, mitigation, and the role of insurance in safeguarding against potential security threats.

4.1 Risk Assessment and Management

4.1.1 Understanding Risk

This section provides an in-depth exploration of what constitutes risk in the context of security economics. It outlines the elements of risk, including threats, vulnerabilities, and consequences, and discusses the concept of risk tolerance.

4.1.2 The Risk Assessment Process

Here, we break down the risk assessment process, which involves identifying, analyzing, evaluating, and prioritizing risks. Special attention is given to methodologies like quantitative and qualitative risk assessment.

4.1.3 Risk Mitigation Strategies

Organizations must decide how to respond to identified risks. This section explores various risk mitigation strategies, such as risk avoidance, risk reduction, risk transfer, and risk acceptance. The economic considerations behind these strategies are elucidated.

## 4.2 The Role of Insurance in Security Economics

### 4.2.1 Security Insurance Basics

This subsection introduces the concept of security insurance, including its purpose and the types of risks it can cover. The economic rationale behind purchasing insurance as a risk management strategy is discussed.

### 4.2.2 Pricing Security Insurance

Understanding how security insurance is priced is crucial. We delve into the factors that influence insurance premiums, including the level of coverage, the organization's risk profile, and market conditions. Actuarial methods and risk modeling are also explained.

### 4.2.3 The Decision to Insure

Organizations must make informed decisions about whether to purchase security insurance. This section explores the economic aspects of this decision, considering factors such as the cost of insurance, potential losses, and risk tolerance.

## 4.3 Case Studies and Examples

Throughout this chapter, real-world case studies and examples illustrate how organizations have effectively managed security risks and used insurance as a risk transfer mechanism. These cases provide insights into the economic implications of different risk management strategies.

## 4.4 Emerging Trends in Security Risk Management

### 4.4.1 Cyber Risk Insurance

With the increasing prevalence of cyber threats, the market for cyber risk insurance has grown significantly. This section explores the economic dynamics of cyber risk insurance and how it addresses the unique challenges of the digital age.

### 4.4.2 Supply Chain Risk Management

Global supply chains face a multitude of risks, and disruptions can have severe economic consequences. We examine how organizations are incorporating risk management and insurance into their supply chain strategies.

### 4.4.3 Climate and Environmental Risk

Climate change and environmental factors pose new risks to organizations. This part of the chapter discusses the economic considerations of managing climate-related risks and the emergence of environmental insurance products.

## 4.5 Conclusion

Chapter 4 concludes by emphasizing the central role of risk management and insurance in security economics. It underscores the economic imperatives behind identifying, assessing, and mitigating risks effectively, as well as considering insurance as a vital tool for transferring risk. As we progress through the book, subsequent chapters will explore additional facets of security economics, including investment strategies, security regulation, and the economic impacts of emerging security trends.

# 5

# Investment Strategies for Security

This chapter delves into the strategies organizations employ to allocate resources for security effectively. Security economics provides a structured framework for determining how much to invest in security measures, weighing the potential returns on investment, and balancing security needs with broader business objectives.

5.1 Allocating Resources for Security

5.1.1 Resource Constraints

This section highlights the resource limitations organizations face when allocating budgets for security. It discusses the need for cost-effective strategies to maximize the impact of security investments.

5.1.2 Risk-Based Approach

A risk-based approach to resource allocation is at the core of security economics. This approach involves identifying and prioritizing security risks based on their potential impact and likelihood, guiding organizations in allocating resources where they are needed most.

### 5.1.3 Balancing Security and Business Objectives

Security is not an end in itself but a means to support business objectives. This subsection explores the delicate balance between security measures and the pursuit of broader organizational goals, emphasizing the economic trade-offs involved.

## 5.2 ROI and Security Investments

### 5.2.1 Return on Investment (ROI) in Security

ROI is a key metric in security economics. It involves assessing the financial returns generated by security investments compared to the initial costs. This section explains how to calculate and interpret ROI in the context of security.

### 5.2.2 Challenges in Measuring Security ROI

Measuring the ROI of security measures can be complex due to various factors, including intangible benefits and long-term impacts. We explore these challenges and present methodologies for overcoming them.

### 5.2.3 The Time Value of Money

Considering the time value of money is essential when evaluating security investments. This subsection introduces concepts like net present value (NPV) and discounted cash flow analysis, which help organizations assess the present value of future security benefits.

## 5.3 Strategies for Effective Security Investments

### 5.3.1 Proactive vs. Reactive Security Measures

Organizations must decide between proactive measures that prevent security incidents and reactive measures that respond to incidents after they occur. This section discusses the economic considerations behind these choices.

### 5.3.2 Security Technology Investments

Investing in security technologies is a common strategy, but it must be done thoughtfully. We explore how organizations can assess the economic value of security technologies, taking into account factors like total cost of ownership and expected benefits.

### 5.3.3 Security as a Competitive Advantage

Security can be a competitive advantage when managed strategically. This part of the chapter discusses how organizations can use security as a selling point to gain customer trust and attract business partners.

## 5.4 Case Studies and Examples

Throughout the chapter, real-world case studies and examples illustrate how organizations have implemented different investment strategies for security. These cases provide insights into the economic considerations that influenced their decisions.

## 5.5 Future Trends in Security Investment

### 5.5.1 Security in Emerging Technologies

As technology evolves, new security challenges and opportunities arise. This section explores the economic implications of security investments in emerging technologies like IoT, AI, and quantum computing.

### 5.5.2 Security in a Remote Work Environment

The shift to remote work has altered the security landscape. We examine how organizations are adapting their security investment strategies in response to this trend and the economic factors driving these changes.

### 5.5.3 The Role of Metrics and KPIs

The use of key performance indicators (KPIs) and metrics is becoming increasingly important in security investment decisions. We explore how organizations are leveraging data and metrics to make more informed and economically sound security investments.

## 5.6 Conclusion

Chapter 5 concludes by emphasizing the critical role of investment strategies in security economics. It underscores the importance of making data-driven decisions, considering ROI, and aligning security investments with organizational objectives. As we progress through the book, subsequent chapters will explore other facets of security economics, including security regulation, human factors, and the economic aspects of emerging security trends.

# 6

# Regulation and Compliance

This chapter explores the Interplayy between government regulations, industry standards, and the costs and benefits incurred by organizations in their pursuit of security.

6.1 Government Regulations in Security

6.1.1 The Regulatory Landscape

This section provides an overview of the regulatory landscape in security, encompassing data protection laws, industry-specific regulations (e.g., healthcare, finance), and international frameworks (e.g., GDPR, HIPAA). It outlines the role of governments in setting security standards and the economic implications for businesses.

6.1.2 Compliance Costs and Benefits

Meeting regulatory requirements often comes with significant costs. This subsection delves into the economic considerations of compliance, including the expenses related to audits, documentation, and staff training, as well as the potential benefits of regulatory adherence.

### 6.1.3 The Impact of Non-Compliance

Non-compliance with security regulations can result in fines, legal consequences, and reputational damage. This part of the chapter examines the economic consequences of non-compliance and how organizations factor these risks into their decision-making.

## 6.2 Industry Standards and Security

### 6.2.1 Industry Frameworks and Standards

Industry-specific security standards and frameworks (e.g., ISO 27001, NIST) play a crucial role in guiding security practices. This section discusses the economic implications of adopting and adhering to these standards, including certification costs and competitive advantages.

### 6.2.2 Harmonization of Standards

In a globalized world, harmonizing security standards across regions can be economically beneficial. This subsection explores the economic rationale for aligning standards and the challenges organizations face in doing so.

### 6.2.3 Certification and Assurance Costs

Achieving certification or assurance under industry standards can be resource-intensive. We analyze the costs associated with certification processes and their impact on organizations' security budgets.

## 6.3 Compliance Management Strategies

### 6.3.1 Compliance as a Business Driver

Some organizations view compliance as an opportunity to enhance their reputation and gain a competitive edge. This part of the chapter discusses how compliance can be leveraged strategically to create economic value.

6.3.2 Compliance Automation

Automating compliance processes can reduce costs and improve efficiency. We explore the economic benefits of compliance automation solutions and their role in managing compliance-related expenses.

6.3.3 Third-Party Compliance Services

Many organizations rely on third-party services for compliance management. This section examines the economic factors that influence the decision to outsource compliance functions and the potential cost savings.

6.4 Case Studies and Examples

Real-world case studies and examples throughout the chapter showcase how organizations navigate security regulation and compliance from an economic perspective. These cases provide insights into the challenges and benefits of compliance efforts.

6.5 Future Trends in Security Regulation and Compliance

6.5.1 Evolving Regulatory Landscape

Regulations in security are constantly evolving. We discuss the economic impacts of emerging regulations, such as those related to privacy, environmental concerns, and emerging technologies like AI and blockchain.

6.5.2 Regulatory Technology (RegTech)

RegTech solutions are gaining traction as tools to streamline compliance processes. This section explores the economic implications of adopting RegTech solutions and their potential to reduce compliance costs.

6.5.3 Global Data Governance

The globalization of data presents new challenges for data governance and compliance. We examine the economic considerations of complying with cross-border data transfer regulations and data localization requirements.

6.6 Conclusion

Chapter 6 concludes by underscoring the central role of security regulation and compliance in security economics. It highlights how organizations must balance the costs of compliance with the potential benefits of regulatory adherence, while also considering the consequences of non-compliance. As we progress through the book, subsequent chapters will explore other key aspects of security economics, including human factors, security in emerging technologies, and the economic impacts of security breaches.

# 7

# Security in Supply Chains

This chapter explores the economic dimensions of security within supply chains. In today's globalized and interconnected world, supply chains are vulnerable to a variety of threats, making security an essential consideration for businesses. Understanding the economics of securing supply chains is crucial for risk mitigation and effective resource allocation.

7.1 Security Challenges in Supply Chains

7.1.1 The Complex Supply Chain Ecosystem

This section outlines the complexity of modern supply chains, which often span multiple countries and involve numerous stakeholders. It highlights the vulnerabilities that arise from this complexity and the potential economic consequences of supply chain disruptions.

7.1.2 Types of Supply Chain Threats

Supply chains face diverse threats, including physical threats (e.g., theft, natural disasters), cyber threats (e.g., data breaches, ransomware), and geopolitical risks (e.g., trade disputes, sanctions). We explore how these threats can disrupt supply chains and their economic implications.

### 7.1.3 The Role of Resilience

Building supply chain resilience is a critical response to security challenges. We delve into the economic rationale for investing in resilience and how it can mitigate supply chain risks.

## 7.2 Supply Chain Risk Assessment and Management

### 7.2.1 Risk Assessment in Supply Chains

Assessing supply chain risks involves identifying vulnerabilities, evaluating potential threats, and quantifying the economic impact of disruptions. We discuss methodologies for supply chain risk assessment and their role in effective risk management.

### 7.2.2 Strategies for Risk Mitigation

This subsection explores risk mitigation strategies within supply chains, including redundancy, diversification, and the economic trade-offs between cost-efficiency and risk reduction.

### 7.2.3 Supplier Risk Management

Supply chain security is closely tied to the security practices of suppliers and partners. We examine how organizations assess and manage supplier risks from an economic perspective.

## 7.3 Economic Impact of Supply Chain Disruptions

### 7.3.1 Direct Costs of Disruptions

When disruptions occur, they come with immediate direct costs, such as production delays, increased transportation costs, and lost sales. This section explores how these costs impact a company's bottom line.

### 7.3.2 Indirect Costs and Reputational Damage

Beyond direct costs, supply chain disruptions can result in indirect costs like damage to reputation and loss of customer trust. We discuss the economic significance of these intangible factors.

### 7.3.3 Long-Term Consequences

Supply chain disruptions can have lasting economic consequences, including changes in customer behavior and long-term damage to relationships with suppliers and partners. We analyze the long-term economic implications of supply chain disruptions.

## 7.4 Case Studies and Examples

Throughout this chapter, real-world case studies and examples illustrate how organizations have tackled supply chain security challenges from an economic perspective. These cases provide insights into the economic considerations that influence supply chain security strategies.

## 7.5 Future Trends in Supply Chain Security Economics

### 7.5.1 Digital Transformation in Supply Chains

The increasing digitization of supply chains introduces new security considerations. We explore the economic impacts of digital transformation on supply chain security.

### 7.5.2 Environmental and Sustainable Supply Chains

Sustainability and environmental concerns are becoming integral to supply chain management. We discuss the economic dimensions of sustainable supply chains and the economic incentives for environmentally responsible practices.

7.5.3 Reshoring and Nearshoring Trends

Recent trends in reshoring and nearshoring are driven by security and economic considerations. We examine the economic factors influencing these decisions and their impact on supply chain security.

7.6 Conclusion

Chapter 7 concludes by emphasizing the importance of supply chain security in the broader context of security economics. It underscores the economic rationale for investing in supply chain security, risk assessment, and resilience-building. As we progress through the book, subsequent chapters will explore other facets of security economics, including human factors, security in emerging technologies, and the economic impacts of security breaches.

# 8

# Human Factors in Security Economics

This chapter delves into the critical role that human factors play in the realm of security economics. Human behavior, decision-making, and workforce training are essential components of effective security, and understanding their economic implications is crucial for organizations.

8.1 Behavioral Economics and Security

8.1.1 Introduction to Behavioral Economics

This section provides an overview of behavioral economics and how it applies to security. It introduces concepts like bounded rationality, cognitive biases, and prospect theory, which influence human decision-making in security contexts.

8.1.2 Behavioral Biases in Security

We explore the various behavioral biases that impact security decisions, including overconfidence, availability bias, and the endowment effect. Understanding these biases is essential for designing security policies and interventions.

### 8.1.3 Economic Impacts of Behavioral Biases

Behavioral biases can have economic consequences, such as increased vulnerability to phishing attacks or resistance to security measures. This part of the chapter discusses how these biases affect security costs and outcomes.

## 8.2 Training and Awareness Programs

### 8.2.1 The Role of Training and Awareness

Training and awareness programs are critical for mitigating human-related security risks. This section examines the economic justification for investing in employee education and awareness campaigns.

### 8.2.2 Costs of Training

Training programs come with costs, including the expenses related to curriculum development, trainers, and employee time. We analyze these costs and their impact on security budgets.

### 8.2.3 Measuring the Effectiveness of Training

Measuring the effectiveness of training is essential for assessing its economic value. We explore methods for evaluating the impact of training programs on security outcomes and cost savings.

## 8.3 Employee Costs vs. Security Gains

### 8.3.1 Balancing Employee Productivity and Security

Balancing the need for security with employee productivity is a delicate economic consideration. This subsection discusses how overly restrictive security measures can impact productivity and competitiveness.

### 8.3.2 The Cost of Insider Threats

Insider threats, whether intentional or accidental, can be costly for organizations. We analyze the economic implications of insider threats and explore strategies for prevention and detection.

### 8.3.3 Motivating Secure Behavior

Incentives and disincentives can influence employee behavior. This part of the chapter delves into the economics of designing incentive structures that motivate secure behavior.

## 8.4 Case Studies and Examples

Real-world case studies and examples throughout the chapter illustrate how organizations have addressed human factors in security economics. These cases provide insights into the economic considerations that shape security training and awareness initiatives.

## 8.5 Future Trends in Human-Centric Security Economics

### 8.5.1 The Role of Artificial Intelligence (AI) in Behavioral Analysis

AI is increasingly used for analyzing and predicting human behavior in security contexts. We explore the economic impacts of AI-driven behavioral analysis and its potential for improving security outcomes.

### 8.5.2 Privacy and Ethical Considerations

Balancing security with privacy and ethical concerns is becoming more complex. We discuss the economic implications of addressing these considerations and their impact on security policies.

### 8.5.3 Remote and Hybrid Workforces

The shift to remote and hybrid workforces presents new security challenges. We examine the economic factors influencing security strategies for distributed work environments.

### 8.6 Conclusion

Chapter 8 concludes by emphasizing the critical role of human factors in security economics. It underscores how human behavior, training, and awareness programs are integral to security decision-making and cost management. As we progress through the book, subsequent chapters will explore other facets of security economics, including security in emerging technologies, regulatory compliance, and the economic impacts of security breaches.

# 9

# Security in the Internet of Things (IoT)

This chapter explores the intricate relationship between security economics and the Internet of Things (IoT). As the IoT continues to proliferate, understanding the economic dimensions of securing interconnected devices and systems becomes increasingly crucial.

9.1 Economics of IoT Security

9.1.1 Introduction to IoT Security Economics

This section introduces the central themes of the chapter by explaining the unique security challenges posed by the IoT. It outlines how economic factors influence IoT security decision-making.

9.1.2 The Expanding IoT Ecosystem

The IoT ecosystem includes a vast array of interconnected devices, from smart home gadgets to industrial sensors. We examine the economic implications of securing this expansive and diverse ecosystem.

9.1.3 Cost-Benefit Analysis in IoT Security

Applying cost-benefit analysis (CBA) to IoT security is essential for making informed decisions about security investments. This part of the chapter discusses the challenges and methodologies involved in performing CBA for IoT security.

## 9.2 IoT Security Challenges and Threats

### 9.2.1 Unique IoT Security Challenges

IoT devices have unique characteristics, such as resource constraints and diverse use cases, that present distinctive security challenges. We explore these challenges and their economic implications.

### 9.2.2 Threat Landscape in the IoT

The IoT is not immune to a wide range of cyber threats. This section discusses the economic motivations of threat actors targeting IoT devices and the potential financial impact of IoT security breaches.

### 9.2.3 Liability and Legal Considerations

Legal and liability issues are paramount in IoT security. We delve into the economic consequences of legal actions and liabilities resulting from security incidents involving IoT devices.

## 9.3 Strategies for IoT Security Economics

### 9.3.1 Risk-Based IoT Security

A risk-based approach is critical in prioritizing IoT security measures. We explore how organizations can economically assess IoT-related risks and allocate resources accordingly.

### 9.3.2 Security by Design

Building security into IoT devices from the design phase can yield economic benefits in the long run. This part of the chapter discusses the economic rationale for implementing security by design principles.

### 9.3.3 IoT Security Standards and Regulations

IoT security standards and regulations are emerging to address the unique challenges of the IoT ecosystem. We analyze the economic considerations of complying with these standards and the potential competitive advantages.

## 9.4 Case Studies and Examples

Throughout the chapter, real-world case studies and examples illustrate how organizations have approached IoT security from an economic perspective. These cases provide insights into the economic considerations that shape IoT security strategies.

## 9.5 Future Trends in IoT Security Economics

### 9.5.1 Edge Computing and IoT Security

Edge computing is becoming integral to IoT architectures. We explore the economic implications of securing IoT data and operations at the edge.

### 9.5.2 Blockchain and IoT Security

Blockchain technology is being explored as a means to enhance IoT security. We discuss the economic aspects of blockchain-based IoT security solutions and their potential benefits.

### 9.5.3 IoT Security as a Service (IoTSecaaS)

As IoT security complexity grows, the emergence of IoTSecaaS is noteworthy. We examine the economic considerations of outsourcing IoT security functions and the potential cost efficiencies.

9.6 Conclusion

Chapter 9 concludes by highlighting the indispensable role of security economics in navigating the complexities of IoT security. It emphasizes how organizations must consider the economics of securing a vast and interconnected array of devices to effectively manage IoT-related risks and investments. As we progress through the book, subsequent chapters will explore other facets of security economics, including security regulation, emerging security trends, and the economic impacts of security breaches.

# 10

# Economic Impacts of Security Breaches

This chapter delves into the profound economic consequences that result from security breaches. It examines how cyberattacks, data breaches, and security incidents affect organizations financially, operationally, and reputationally.

## 10.1 The Cost of Security Breaches

### 10.1.1 Direct Financial Costs

Security breaches often come with immediate financial costs, including expenses related to incident response, forensic investigations, and legal fees. This section explores how these direct costs impact an organization's bottom line.

### 10.1.2 Indirect Costs

Beyond the direct financial impact, security breaches can result in indirect costs. We discuss how factors such as business disruption, loss of customer trust, and increased insurance premiums contribute to the overall economic burden.

### 10.1.3 Long-Term Financial Consequences

Security breaches can have lasting financial consequences, including ongoing security investments, loss of business opportunities, and damage to market value. We analyze the long-term economic implications of security incidents.

## 10.2 Measuring the Economic Impact

### 10.2.1 Methodologies for Impact Assessment

Measuring the economic impact of security breaches is complex. This subsection explores various methodologies, including cost estimation models, to quantify the financial repercussions of breaches.

### 10.2.2 Challenges in Impact Assessment

Assessing the economic impact of breaches faces challenges, including the difficulty of quantifying intangible losses. We discuss the limitations and best practices in impact assessment.

### 10.2.3 The Role of Insurance

Insurance plays a role in mitigating the economic impact of breaches. We explore how organizations leverage cyber insurance to transfer financial risks and reduce the overall cost of security incidents.

## 10.3 Reputational Damage and Customer Trust

### 10.3.1 Reputation as a Valuable Asset

A strong reputation is a valuable intangible asset for organizations. We examine the economic significance of reputational damage resulting from security breaches.

### 10.3.2 Measuring Reputational Damage

Quantifying the reputational damage caused by breaches is challenging but essential. We discuss methodologies for assessing reputational impact and the potential economic consequences of tarnished brands.

### 10.3.3 Rebuilding Customer Trust

Rebuilding customer trust is critical after a breach. This section explores the economic considerations behind investing in trust-building strategies and their long-term financial benefits.

## 10.4 Regulatory and Legal Consequences

### 10.4.1 Legal Costs and Liabilities

Security breaches often lead to legal actions and liabilities. We analyze the economic implications of legal expenses, fines, and settlements resulting from breaches.

### 10.4.2 Compliance and Regulatory Costs

Compliance with data protection regulations is essential after a breach. We discuss the economic costs of complying with regulatory requirements and the potential impacts on an organization's financial health.

### 10.4.3 Class Action Lawsuits

Class action lawsuits can have substantial financial repercussions. This part of the chapter explores the economic aspects of defending against and settling class action suits.

## 10.5 Case Studies and Examples

Real-world case studies and examples throughout the chapter illustrate how organizations have grappled with the economic consequences of security breaches. These cases provide insights into the financial, reputational, and legal considerations that shape breach response strategies.

10.6 Future Trends in Breach Economics

10.6.1 The Cost of Data Privacy

As data privacy concerns grow, organizations face increasing pressure to protect sensitive information. We explore the economic factors driving investments in data privacy and the potential return on these investments.

10.6.2 Ransomware Economics

Ransomware attacks have become prevalent. We analyze the economic dynamics of ransomware, including ransom payments, recovery costs, and prevention strategies.

10.6.3 The Role of Cybersecurity Insurance

The cybersecurity insurance market is evolving. We discuss how this market is adapting to the changing threat landscape and the economic considerations of purchasing cyber insurance.

10.7 Conclusion

Chapter 10 concludes by emphasizing the far-reaching economic implications of security breaches. It underscores how organizations must not only invest in preventive measures but also consider the economic dimensions of breach response, reputation management, and compliance to effectively navigate the aftermath of security incidents. As we conclude the book, we reflect on the multifaceted nature of security economics and its critical role in shaping security strategies and decision-making.

# 11

# Emerging Trends in Security Economics

This chapter explores the dynamic and ever-evolving landscape of security economics, highlighting emerging trends and their potential economic impacts. Understanding these trends is essential for organizations to adapt and make informed decisions in an increasingly complex security environment.

11.1 The Evolving Threat Landscape

11.1.1 Sophistication of Cyber Threats

Cyber threats continue to grow in sophistication and complexity. This section discusses the economic implications of combating advanced threats and the need for continuous investment in security.

11.1.2 Nation-State Threat Actors

Nation-state-sponsored cyberattacks pose unique challenges. We explore the economic motivations behind state-sponsored hacking and the potential consequences for targeted organizations.

11.1.3 The Dark Web and Cybercrime Economy

The dark web has become a thriving marketplace for cybercriminals. We delve into the economics of cybercrime, including the sale of stolen data and hacking tools, and its impact on organizations.

## 11.2 Security Automation and Artificial Intelligence (AI)

### 11.2.1 Automating Security Operations

Automation and AI are transforming security operations. This subsection discusses the economic benefits of automating routine tasks and leveraging AI for threat detection and response.

### 11.2.2 The Role of Machine Learning

Machine learning algorithms play a crucial role in security analytics. We explore the economic aspects of implementing machine learning for anomaly detection and predictive analysis.

### 11.2.3 The Economics of Security Orchestration

Security orchestration and automation platforms (SOAR) are gaining traction. We discuss the economic considerations of adopting SOAR solutions to streamline incident response.

## 11.3 Cloud Security and Migration

### 11.3.1 Cloud Security Economics

As organizations migrate to the cloud, they must assess the economics of cloud security. This section explores the cost implications of securing cloud environments and data.

### 11.3.2 Security as a Service (SECaaS)

Security as a Service is becoming a prevalent model. We examine the economic rationale for outsourcing security functions to third-party providers and the potential cost efficiencies.

### 11.3.3 Cloud Compliance and Governance

Ensuring compliance in the cloud has economic implications. We discuss the costs associated with maintaining compliance and the risks of non-compliance.

## 11.4 Privacy and Data Protection

### 11.4.1 The Economics of Data Privacy

Data privacy regulations continue to evolve. We explore the economic factors driving investments in data protection and the potential economic consequences of data breaches.

### 11.4.2 Privacy by Design

Privacy by design principles are gaining prominence. We discuss the economic incentives for integrating privacy considerations into product and service development.

### 11.4.3 Cross-Border Data Transfers

Cross-border data transfer regulations impact global organizations. We examine the economic considerations of complying with these regulations and the potential disruptions to data flows.

## 11.5 Geopolitical and Regulatory Influences

### 11.5.1 Geopolitical Tensions and Cybersecurity

Geopolitical conflicts can spill over into cyberspace. We analyze the economic consequences of cybersecurity in a geopolitically charged world.

### 11.5.2 Expanding Security Regulations

Security regulations are on the rise. We explore the economic impacts of complying with an expanding landscape of security and data protection regulations.

### 11.5.3 The Role of Public-Private Partnerships

Public-private partnerships in cybersecurity are growing. We discuss the economic benefits of collaborative efforts to address shared security challenges.

## 11.6 Conclusion

Chapter 11 concludes by emphasizing the continuous evolution of security economics and the need for organizations to adapt to emerging trends. It underscores the economic considerations that shape decisions in an ever-changing security landscape and the importance of staying informed and agile to effectively manage security risks and investments. As we conclude this book, we reflect on the dynamic nature of security economics and its pivotal role in safeguarding organizations in the digital age.

# 12

# Strategic Decision-Making in Security Economics

This final chapter serves as a capstone to the exploration of security economics. It focuses on strategic decision-making within organizations, integrating the various aspects of security economics discussed throughout the book and providing guidance on how to develop a comprehensive security strategy that balances economic considerations with security imperatives.

12.1 Security as a Business Enabler

12.1.1 Aligning Security with Business Objectives

Effective security economics involves aligning security strategies with broader organizational goals. This section discusses how security can serve as a business enabler and create economic value.

12.1.2 The Role of Security Leadership

Security leaders play a critical role in driving the alignment of security with business objectives. We explore the economic benefits of strong security leadership and the impact on decision-making.

### 12.1.3 Building a Security-Centric Culture

Creating a security-centric organizational culture is vital. This subsection discusses the economic implications of fostering a culture that prioritizes security awareness and compliance.

## 12.2 Resource Allocation and Risk Management

### 12.2.1 Balancing Security Investments

Resource allocation is a fundamental aspect of security economics. We delve into the economic trade-offs involved in allocating resources to different security measures.

### 12.2.2 Risk-Based Decision-Making

A risk-based approach guides resource allocation. We discuss how organizations can use risk assessment and cost-benefit analysis to make informed decisions about security investments.

### 12.2.3 Dynamic Resource Allocation

The security landscape is dynamic. We examine the economic considerations of adjusting resource allocation in response to evolving threats and vulnerabilities.

## 12.3 Security Governance and Compliance

### 12.3.1 Governance Frameworks

Establishing robust governance frameworks is essential. We discuss the economic benefits of implementing governance structures that ensure security compliance and accountability.

### 12.3.2 Regulatory Compliance

Compliance with security regulations is non-negotiable. We explore how organizations can navigate the economic complexities of meeting regulatory requirements while managing costs.

### 12.3.3 Third-Party Risk Management

Managing third-party security risks is a growing concern. This section discusses the economic implications of vendor risk assessments and strategies for cost-effective third-party risk management.

## 12.4 Resilience and Incident Response

### 12.4.1 Building Resilience

Resilience is an economic imperative in security. We analyze the costs and benefits of resilience-building efforts that help organizations withstand security incidents.

### 12.4.2 Incident Response Planning

Effective incident response is cost-efficient. We explore the economic advantages of having well-defined incident response plans and capabilities.

### 12.4.3 Post-Incident Recovery

Recovery after a security incident involves costs. This subsection discusses the economic considerations of post-incident recovery efforts and their impact on organizational continuity.

## 12.5 Monitoring and Adaptation

### 12.5.1 Continuous Monitoring

Continuous monitoring is essential for staying ahead of security threats. We discuss the economic advantages of real-time monitoring and threat intelligence.

### 12.5.2 Adapting to Emerging Trends

Adaptation is key to security resilience. We explore how organizations can economically adapt to emerging security trends and technologies.

### 12.5.3 Security Metrics and Key Performance Indicators (KPIs)

Metrics and KPIs play a vital role in monitoring and adaptation. We discuss the economic significance of using data-driven metrics to assess security performance.

## 12.6 Conclusion: A Holistic Approach to Security Economics

Chapter 12 concludes by emphasizing the need for organizations to take a holistic approach to security economics. It underscores the importance of integrating security considerations into every aspect of organizational decision-making, from resource allocation to risk management to resilience-building. This comprehensive approach enables organizations to address security challenges effectively while considering the economic factors that impact their bottom line. As we conclude this book, we reflect on the enduring relevance of security economics as a critical discipline for the digital age.

www.ingramcontent.com/pod-product-compliance
Lightning Source LLC
Chambersburg PA
CBHW060034040426
42333CB00042B/2438